POETRY NOW

A WORLD AT WAR

Edited by Kerrie Pateman

First published in Great Britain in 1994 by
POETRY NOW
1-2 Wainman Road, Woodston,
Peterborough, PE2 7BU

FOREWORD

Although we are a nation of poetry writers we are accused of not reading poetry and not buying poetry books: after many years of listening to the incessant gripes of poetry publishers, I can only assume that the books they publish, in general, are books that most people do not want to read.

Poetry should not be obscure, introverted, and as cryptic as a crossword puzzle: it is the poet's duty to reach out and embrace the world.

The world owes the poet nothing and we should not be expected to dig and delve into a rambling discourse searching for some inner meaning.

The reason we write poetry (and almost all of us do) is because we want to communicate: an ideal; an idea; or a specific feeling. Poetry is as essential in communication, as a letter; a radio; a telephone, and the main criteria for selecting the poems in this anthology is very simple: they communicate.

Faced with hundreds of poems and a limited amount of space, the task of choosing the final poems was difficult and as editor one tries to be as detached as possible (quite often editors can become a barrier in the writer-reader exchange) acting as go between, making the connection, not censoring because of personal taste.

In this volume around one hundred and thirty poems are presented to the reader for their enjoyment.

The poetry is written on all levels; the simple and the complex both having their own appeal.

The success of this collection, and all previous *Poetry Now* anthologies, relies on the fact that there are as many individual readers as there are writers, and in the diversity of styles and forms there really is something to please, excite, and hopefully, inspire everyone who reads the book.

CONTENTS

RETURN OF THE VETERANS

We stood in solemn silence there
The name on the grave reminded us
We're back in Normandy
And all the world is no mite wiser yet.

We have the lines of three score years and ten
But we were eighteen years old then
We've learned a lot but not forgot
You and I.

The Sky's the same we remember
We looked at such a sky long ago
Human nature and sky's don't change
yet all the world is no mite wiser yet.

We had to come back
Before we follow those we left here
They died that we might live! To us a myth
You and I.

We wonder why
Why young men are easily led to kill each other?
We were the same
Who can we blame?

The world would be a better place we thought
It isn't though we fought
We know that all the wars ever won
Improved the world not one crumb.

If we could resurrect the soldiers dead
And show them what they've missed
We doubt they'd thank us for the glimpse
Yet all the world is no mite wiser yet.

C O Burnell

MEMORIES

In quiet retrospection,
as we dip in memories store.
A Kaleidoscope of happenings,
we find there by the score.
Echoes of childish escapades,
with Tommy, Jane, or Jill.
Remembered faces, now long gone,
a house upon a hill.

Memories of youth and Springtime,
the hopes, the dreams, and fears.
Of young men going off to war,
the long and anxious years.
Women in the factories, on the farms,
and in the forces.
The blackouts, and the rationing,
and sharing of resources.

Evacuated children came from towns,
into the country.
Hugging gas-masks, bags and toys,
received by all and sundry.
Lost, bewildered little ones,
whose tears were soon to melt,
And older ones, who settled down
to make their presence felt.

With peace then won, the men returned,
who'd fought to fend the cause
Though many more were left behind,
to rest on foreign shores.
But life goes on, and memory brings
the sound of wedding bell,
And youthful dreams were now fulfilled,
to long frustrations quell.

Memory, like a patchwork quilt,
built up of recollections,
Is one in which we all hold store,
a stock of vast collections.
Joyous, funny, poignant too,
to summon when inclined,
Are memories spanning all the years,
a treasury of mind.

M E Ireland

THE KHAKI AND THE GREY

The poppy seeds that dormant lay,
As the cosmic clock ticks on,
Beneath the peaceful harvest field,
'Midst the Khaki and the Grey,
Rotting now to fertile dust
From conflict long long gone.

Tread lightly on this hallowed ground,
In a strange and foreign land,
Recall again that bloodied past,
With the silence now around.
Ponder then, on the Khaki and the Grey,
Lying, unknown, in blood soaked clay and sand.

Generations are bom, then pass,
The seeds awake, and poppies grow,
Through the Khaki and the Grey,
To the lush and thickening grass,
Toward the blinding daytime light,
And the evenings' golden glow.

From immortal seeds they've grown,
To beautify, delight,
Full bloom in summers lengthening day,
Above the soil of those unknown,
Blood red for eternal remembrance,
Of the Khaki and the Grey.

Iolo Lewis

UNTITLED

Standing there midst great array
To commemorate Remembrance Day
Medals proudly pinned to their chests
King and Country they had gave the best
On foreign shores and ocean's deep
They fought to keep their country free
To honour comrades who lost their lives
So democracy would still survive
Whilst on their shoulders bore the brunt
Don't lets forget our own home front
Housewives who worked on shop floors
Land army girls who toiled outdoors
Fire fighters those boys in blue
Who often gave their lives too
To fight the blitz of bombs and flames
That from the skies at night did rain
Mining folk who dug out the coal
To keep our factories in full flow
Alongside they did employ
Lads they called the Bevin Boys
No medals and ribbons for their chests
But they served their country like the rest

D Ryan

THE MEMORIAL

There's a memorial in our village.
To the lads who fought and fell,
In two great Wars, so long ago.
Where they shared a life like hell.

There's a memorial in our village.
And perhaps its just as well,
That the mums and dads of those brave lads,
Are no longer here to tell!

Of how it has been neglected,
With dirt and weeds all round.
It should be more respected,
It is on hallowed ground.

I went up to the council,
Just to air my views,
But the words of an old soldier,
To them, was just bad news.

They said that money was short,
There wasn't any spare,
To pay someone to clean it up,
So no one seemed to care.

But when armistice day comes round.
It will be quite spick and span.
So they can come and lay their wreath.
As we old veterans can.

And in the moments silence.
I hope they will recall.
That while we are here, to share our lives each day
Those brave lads gave their all.

Harry Slaney

ARNHEM LIFT

A Sunday morning, bright and clear
  In autumn's misty glow,
The sound of droning aircraft
  Disturbs the quiet below!

The powered aircraft's pulsing hum
  The Gliders towed behind,
A sight so wondrous, fearful too,
  Whose mission secrets bind.

How could we know these brave young men
  With courage in that hour,
Turned to Commandos when cast off
  They landed without power.

No-one could know the hope sustained -
  Would Arnhem end the war?
And, if not, how could they be risked?
  The hopes of all could soar!

'Twas not to be, though gallantly
  They faced the Panzers' might
Enduring more than humans should
  They stood alone to fight!

A few came back, much eager youth
  Was lost on Holland's shore,
I always hoped, my pilot *did*
  Return to me once more!

Betty Simpson

THE INFANTRYMAN

All truth, within itself hides truth,
  And fallacy - truth's dust, conceals:
The mirrored distance, often vague
  Appears.
Wisdom's eyes must judge the present,
  In the learning of the past;
That all things seen are temporal,
  The unseen truths that last.

When Death and Hate play chessmen,
  With countless human pawns -
The indiscriminating metal seeks
  Its goal.
The inner self deactivates,
  The outer, boldness shows;
The eyes alone can tell the fear,
  That only courage knows.

Too scared to be a coward,
  Too frightened to be brave;
The iron strings of discipline
  Control.
Opinions forming sterile
  On a tongue that must not speak;
The unshed tear rejected, as
  A symbol of the weak.

Heart thumping, hollow, drum-like,
  High in a parched throat;
Belly, wild and twisted sour, in
  Convulsions.
The body waits the Order -
  To follow, ranks demands.
The mind rebels - protective;
  The mind no more commands.

Words of gratitude and glory,
  Uttered in a moment's praise,
Recount the steadfast sacrifice
  Of Duty.
In the secret of the inner heart
  The unshed tear that shows;
The unshed tear of truth reminds
  The fear that courage knows.

M R M Pattison

OH, WHAT A LOVELY WAR

Not a First Night heart remained unmoved.
The elderly rubbed their bruises of recollection,
Mourned afresh behind their laughter,
Saw the tarnished glory in perspective,
Smothering the sob of futility
With the fireburst of their applause.
The solemn-eyed appraisal of the young
Offered an undisclosed opinion
That might have awed us by the lucid
Simplicity of its reasoning.
We never pried for their reactions,
Yet their incandescence strangely chastened us.
We, who were children in the Second War,
Whose grandparents talked of Flanders fields,
The grisly mayhem of trench warfare,
The enduring agony of gas,
We wear our own poppies of retrospect.
Our war was evacuee labels,
Anderson shelters, the siren's shivering tremor
Across stricken classrooms.
We danced, pierrot-like, upon the boards
Of experience beyond our years.
Even now, the white cliffs of Dover
Chill us with eerie innuendoes of invasion . . .

Joan B Howes

TWO FRIENDS REMEMBERED

Ex-Cobridge choirboy, home on leave,
Three hard-earned stripes upon his sleeve
Above his heart wings newly won
And much admired by everyone.
Though wet and windy, none too warm,
Greatcoat was carried on his arm:
Bill palpably declined to hide
The pilots' badge he wore with pride.

Commissioned later, justly so,
A pilot officer who'd know
No further opportunity
Of climbing the promotion tree.
Killed much too soon, aircraft aflame,
Like Icarus to earth he came.
And his reward for gallantry?
Nought save the tears of family.

Ex-Cobridge choirboy, we recall
Jack's first appearance: rather small,
Round, rosy cheeks, a cheerful grin,
A dimpled cleft beneath his chin.
An inoffensive innocent
Whose love of life was evident.
No indication then that he
Possessed heroic quality.

We subsequently lost all trace
Until we read of time and place,
Of how he faced the Hun's attack
Withstood their onslaught, held them back
Alone, unaided, wounded sore.
The hopeless odds chose to ignore,
And his reward for gallantry?
Victoria Cross, posthumously.

Howard Cooke

1944 ODE TO 928 (BALLOON) SQUADRON RAF

Felixstowe is a well known RAF station,
That's noted for binding and bull,
'Twas the homestead of 928 Squadron
Where most lived their lives to the full.

They deflated the *bladders* one evening
and posted the men by the score,
and sent them to catch Hitler's buzz bombs,
as here they were needed no more

But a few of us were forgotten,
We are having a terrible life,
For we know we're not wanted in Coastal,
And all is but trouble and strife.

One WAAF is driving the coal truck,
and gets all smothered with dust,
and although she is *mad* she is harmless,
and obey Station Orders she must.

Another was sent to Headquarters,
And if in the window you peep,
You'll see there a big heap of papers,
And under - this girl asleep.

Are we poor stoogies forgotten?
Is it true we are no more to roam,
if that is the case we'll start packing,
and fly like *Doodlebugs* home

But lo on the last of November,
All hurry and scurry were we,
We are leaving 928 Squadron,
And saying goodbye to the sea.

The powers that be, have decided,
that without us they can't win the war,
so theyare packing us off to Stanmore
where we can be useful once more.

L K Newling Ex Sgt. RAFUR

BURMA IN THE MOONLIGHT (A TRUE LOVE POEM)

Burma in the moonlight . . .
Stars, like lanterns hanging low -
A *Zero* turning on the wing,
While in the twilight glow
Of early evening in Rangoon -
A Burmese girl stands waiting
For her lover . . . who would soon
Declare his love . . . then fly no more,
But stay a hero in her eyes
Long after all the violence
Had vanished from the skies,
And all the US planes had gone . . .
And Burma breathed once more -

Such was her tale in Mingladon,
A tale of love . . . a tale of war . . .

I listened, knowing only I
Would ever share her grief
And know the pain of war-time love -
A love so sweet . . . a love so brief!

Burma in the moonlight . . .
A *Zero* on the wing,
A Burmese girl looks up and sighs -
Remembering . . . remembering . . . !

Russell Humphrey

A WORLD AT WAR

It was in the year of thirty nine,
That Germany ran out of time,
So once more to war we go,
Once more against the same old foe,
Will it be a quick affair,
No-one can trust them over there,
So sandbag filling must be done,
While enjoying the September sun.

Young men joined recruiting queues,
Mum listens for the wireless news,
Some do a stint after factory work,
This wasn't the time for us to shirk,
When our allies gave up the fight,
Our troops were left in desperate plight,
The small ships then sailed for France,
And gave many soldiers a second chance.

Now in the Home Guard dad parades,
With his Lee Enfield to foil any raids,
But the enemy do not try,
Still our men were on standby,
Now the bombers come at night,
And on civilians released their might,
Our young girls now man the guns,
Firing their shells at bombing Huns.

The ARP were on the ball,
Helping people as buildings fall,
Fighting fires on the edge of hell,
Heroes were in their personnel,
Now the world has joined the fight,
And across the Channel sails our might,
With bitter fighting the enemy runs,
But we have lost many of our sons.

Bernard T Phillips

THEY'VE DISAPPEARED?

The tramping of feet,
On the roads into hell,
The screaming of orders,
And our battle cry yells.

The death rattle, of guns,
As the mortar bombs fell,
The revving of tanks
On this road into hell.

The streets lined with bodies
With the wounded that fell,
The smoke and the fires
We were stokers in hell.

Blood on the ceilings
Blood on the floors
Blood on the walls,
We can't take a lot more.

Praying and hoping,
For, 2nd Armies tanks roar,
Please make an effort
We can't take it much more.

The burning of flesh,
The smells in the air,
The thunderous sounds,
Congealed blood everywhere.

Abandoned in Arnhem,
On this road into hell,
With tanks all around us,
We fought, till we fell.

Norrie Hill

AND STILL IN FIELDS . . .

Of those who were young when we were young
But who died in the battles and cities of war
Would many still say, those heroes unsung
This was worth fighting for?

I cannot feel pride for those who died.
Those valiant men; they were called to enlist.
And that is our shame. The war-lords' stride
Had threatened for years but we let it exist.

If those men had lived, if no war had waged
Would the wealth lost in war have been used for their good?
Fifty years on their sons, now middle-aged
Have health and learning, shelter and food.

All these as rights. But world peace is a right.
Yet down through the years spreads the chaos of war.
The peak of creation, man must still fight
Our nature still red in tooth and in claw.

But our race has not one head - it is diverse
Millions of people have millions of heads.
If each gave enough thought we'd be rid of war's curse
Of bombs, racism, statelessness, so many dreads.

Could it be that the peaceable speak with quiet voices
While dictators shout and drums call to arms
Till the frenzied pack howls and baseness rejoices
And good men must fight for their homes and their farms?

Is there a way, and might men still find it
Before all is lost, while poppies still grow
While there's still a dove, and a child to see it?
Who can know?

Norma D'Lemos

THE PRICE OF WAR

Have you seen the bitter glory,
When a war drags to an end.
The stillness of death's inventory,
Is noisier than the defeated's pen.

The scratch upon the declaration,
Pen to paper ends a nation,
And all the people torn asunder,
Bloody wars, fought and blundered.

Lost are causes and dreamed of ideals,
Now, a life long court of appeals,
When nations fight for understanding,
Then policies are too demanding.

Then what of deprivation, to exist,
To build your dreams on only broken bits,
Hope is born stronger in each mind,
Brotherhood is also greater, you will find.

But sorrow of the battle honoured dead,
The hopelessness of families that have bled,
When everything you ever had is lost,
And only sweat and tears will pay the cost.

Then comes the trial of seeing the bitter end,
To start living on the road that has no bend,
A light is born within each shattered heart,
The will is kindled, ready for the start.

William Nichol

GIRL SEEN AT A CONVENT IN NORTH ITALY - WINTER 1945

She stood near me
At the service
In the shabby convent

She wore a fur hat
Had a long, worn coat
Tight, snow-flaked boots
And she carried an old muff

She looked like an emaciated character
In a Russian novel -
Anna Karenina possibly

She chanted the responses
Quietly, intensely
But with fervour

She stared at the relics
And the priests
With their brilliant open bibles
And flashing finery
As if by staring hard
She'd receive an extra revelation

Her face
Like the Madonna in the fresco
Was adoring the spectacle
She lit a candle
Who was it for?

In that nunnery
In 1945
In the depth
Of harsh winter
Her breath was like smoke
In the chill nave
The beautiful young woman
From a war-torn world.

John W Dossett-Davies

BEING A SOLDIER

As you are an Englishman
it's as if right from the start
you're destined to be a Soldier,
the Army a vital part;
down through all those ages,
        Agincourt, the Somme,
        South Africa and India,
battles of right or wrong.

When your turn comes
you're mustered, recruited for the fray,
not of your own making,
to hold you, night and day.
So, you take up the musket,
        sword or lance or gun;
        respond to call of duty,
chastened by the drum.

Our fathers fought; they suffered
        at Verdun and Passchendaele,
and we in turn did battle
at Cassino and Grenadier Hill, then
later, in Korea and folly Falklands
fight; fatalists ready to soldier,
and, if need be, forfeit life.

From Private up to General
we're defenders of our realm;
protectors of a sweet land,
        from Corporal to Colonel.
Hearing the last post sounded but
        for so many no reveille;
sleeping on, not seeing their dawn
in distant hill or valley.

Arthur Rowell

INVISIBLE CHILD (OF WAR)

You must have been invisible,
To die, and not be missed,
There must have been someone you loved,
Whose face you touched and kissed,
How could we never notice,
That you were not around,
You must have passed so silently,
Unseen without a sound.

Were you scared as you were dying,
Or more afraid of life,
Was your mother there beside you,
To hold, as breath expired,
And when she heard you crying,
Were her heart and soul destroyed,
Did she feel a rage, and torment,
For the aid that was devoid,
And what about your father,
Did he hurt, that he had failed,
As your guardian, and protector,
When your freedom was assailed,
Was the sorrow and the anguish,
Too much for them to bear,
Did they lose all faith, and future,
In the blackness of despair.

Too late, we feel the need to reach.
To comfort, and to love you,
So our children we must teach,
That your life, and how you lived it,
Was really not your fault,
And our own easy existence, is merely by default.

Deirdre Anne Bates

TARGET. PREDICTOR CONTROL

Target. Predictor control
The tannoy sends its call,
To stations on the guns we race,
Our heartbeats pounding haul
On to target. Sight the guns.
Set the shells and load.
Await command, then fire at will,
Release the case. Reload.
Fire. The crescendo leaps,
All guns discharge their shot.
With gleeful roar they speed away
Following the gunner's plot.
The pretty flares the planes disgorge
Display their solemn glow,
Like chandeliers of fiery torch,
Illumines death below.
The *crump* of bombs, exploding shells,
The searchlight's piercing glow,
Our minds are numbed to scenes around,
The deadly seeds we sow.
And so it rumbles through the night,
We strain to keep abreast,
The droning planes retreat to base,
The *all clear* shrieks its jest.
And now the battle's over,
The shattered earth at bay,
Our sentinels go back on guard,
Peace dawns another day.

Thomas V Healey

HOPE

Where is the honour?
The glory that is wed
To martial strife.
Where immortality?
Given to the dead
In afterlife.
Is it a stone?
Clear-cut with names
In long array.
Is it the crowd?
That's hushed and claims
Remembrance Day.

Unwashed, and thick
With desert dust,
The sand congealed
With clots of blood,
I only feel disgust,
My faith concealed.
I search in vain
For higher things
But find no peace.

Breaks forth the dawn
On bright'ning wings,
And troubles cease.

Andrew Todd

CASUALTIES OF WAR

Her crying was different that night,
Different from the lonely nights before.
Different from the last time she saw him,
When he marched, with the others, off to war.

Each night I could feel her sobbing,
As she lay in the bed next to me.
Come morning things would be fine again
And she'd smile as I climbed on her knee.

But that night, something had altered.
Hushed voices, the door being shut.
A terrible scream made me stiffen,
As fear throbbed and twisted my gut.

My father was naught but a picture,
But mother had taught me his name.
And told me of trips and at Christmas time,
That he would be home once again.

He was more than a picture, to mother.
He'd held her and showed that he cared.
When he wrote and said that he loved her,
She remembered, every last word.

Well, now he had gone, gone forever.
Never more to walk through our door.
He had died in the company of heroes
As they fought upon a French shore.

Even now, I still hear her sobbing,
The memories just won't fade away.
Though I was small, I remember
As if it was just yesterday.

C McCombe

WHERE'ER I SEE THE POPPIES BLOOM

Where'er I see the Poppies bloom
my mind will sadly dwell
On those far distant foreign fields
where the flower of a nation fell.

As swaying gently in the breeze
like wraiths their spirits cast
Caught in the whisperings of the
wind the voices of the past.

I can hear the sound of the
drummer boy, youth innocent of guile
Sense the young man's dream of glory
feel his irrepressible smile.

I play host to the sounds of distant
drums, echoing their torment
To the melancholy strains of the
piper as he plays his sad lament.

I grieve for their light was
dimmed too soon, as the flower
of their youth was sown,
and scattered across the universe
to where the Poppy seeds have grown.

My thoughts disturb the silent
tears of pain, deep in the womb
So shall I remember them
Where ever Poppies bloom.

June Pledger

CASSINO

I saw him pointing with trembling hand
To those unchanging walls;
Pitiless walls that frowned upon
The godlessness of man
And saw him fleshless lie.

I saw his finger in the darkness lift
Towards the crumbling town,
The endless battlements, the monastery on high,
Which like an emperor in the Roman days
Would watch us in that vast arena die.

'There lies the way to Rome,' he said.
And all the ghosts of old who spoke those words
Rose up.

I heard them sigh.

Robin Ivy

TO WILFRED OWEN
FROM THE WESTERN DESERT, 1943

Since you cried out from Flanders' mud, benighted,
And we are Churchill's lads, who oft delighted
On Libyan plains to frolic in the sun,
How dare we speak to you? Your duty done,
You rest. Yet we must also call up ghosts
Who fought, like you, against aggressive hosts.
Our consciences are no more clear than yours,
Our feelings no more cauterised by war's
Catastrophes. So let us, with respect,
Defend our breaking from your peace, reject
A charge implied from your neglected grave.

When Nazis swarmed in vengeance for defeat
Inflicted by the war you suffered, heat
Responded in our minds, a sense of right,
Compelling answer. Losing then the white
Of truce, we felt the red of fierce explosion.
We saw it blast our hopes, and with corrosion
Destroy our palaces of peace. That night
You lived through came again to menace. Bright
The youth we lost, and now we come to you,
Sincere in homage. For we think it true
When world opinion has been fully polled
They'll find we soldiers are not overbold
To march that painful way through war's grim gate
To deal with those who seize by force. So, late,
Reluctant, slow, we have not rushed to kill,
But had to fight, to maintain justice still.

Kenneth Parker

THE GLORY OF WAR

The stench of hot gasoline and burning flesh pervades the air,
offends flared nostrils, as remorselessly the flame throwers
devour all in their path.
In the distance the stark silhouette of a tiger rumbles over the hill.
Trench coated shell shocked eyes once so proud, belie the
tales of glory that are war.

Where is the glory, where is the honour, the grandeur
as wretchedly they cower in their sodden trenches?

A staccato of machine pistol startles the few remaining birds
in the nearby copse, as the once verdant land now a sea of
crimson mud bears testament to the decadence of man.

A pall of black smoke hangs heavy across no-man's land, as the
cry goes out, over the top!
Gangrenous feet trample the putrescent corpse's of fallen
comrades beneath the rat infested mire.

Triumphant, they herd the vanquished back behind the lines,
a chance to rest, to sleep the sleep of the exhausted,
to remember in broken nightmares their mutilated comrades.
White rows of bleak stone now stand where once the poppies grew.

Where is the honour, where is the grandeur, the glory that is war.

T S Hurford

REMEMBRANCE

The muted toll,
The bell of war,
Men of all ages,
Called up score on score,
What does life mean,
Why were they born,
Their lives to be harvested,
Like sheaves of ripe corn.

On fields of cold earth,
Deserts hot with sun,
They shed their life's blood,
So that we could live on,
To war they were called,
Died one by one,
Remember we must,
The ones that live on.

Brave men's spirits,
Will forever remain,
When we see,
Blood red poppies,
And reap in golden grain,
Imagine young faces,
No lines you see there,
They sleep now forever,
Without troubles or care.

Muriel Rodgers

THE MUSTER - D-DAY 50 YEARS ON

Fifth of June, we went down, to the Solent
Anniversary, of a battle, long ago
The Longest Day, its been called, by my elders
On this day, much emotion, was to show.

Was the D, short for death, on this D-Day?
Where so many, were cut down, in their prime
When they leapt, from their craft, on beach landing
For these lads, there was just, no more time.

They lay, where they fell, combat laden
And their blood, stained the sands, washed by sea
Gave all, in this vast, broiling battle
Saved the world, from that Nazi, tyranny.

On this day, fifty years, since that happening
Naval Muster, ships large and small, a thousand boats
Heads of State, led by our Queen, in Britannia
Reviewed the anchored, and the sailing, reviewed the lot.

The day was fine, a freshening breeze, ideal for boating
And they came, by their hundred, the world to see
In line astern, and then abeam, they tracked the convoy
Made us so proud, to be a part, this symphony.

The water boiled, with cut and thrust, of many bowlines
First they were high, then way down, in darker green
To rise again, atop a collar, snow-white and foaming
This was the sight, those soldier boys, should have seen.

Yes we were there, to remember, their achievements
They cast the die, for the future, how it could be
Now up to us, not take for granted, their endeavours
We will remember, and celebrate, Their Victory.

Trevor Perrin

THE OLD SOLDIER

I saw him going, past my door.
Just as I did, the day before.
His suit, tho' neat, was slightly frayed.
No emotion, on his face, displayed.
Who knew, the thoughts, upon his mind?
Or what those, tired old eyes, might find.

I saw him last year, with his wife.
She was the centre of his life.
Hand in hand, along our road,
Coming or going, to their abode.
So proudly, did they show their love,
That seemed, a blessing, from above.

Came the Spring, they passed not my door.
The hour of parting, was in store.
Her life's journey, had spent, its course.
The debt to nature, came into force.
The old man, looked up to the skies,
Tears of love, streamed from his eyes.

How hard it was, to face his loss,
'Twas up to him, to bear that cross.
The world outside, seemed cold and bare.
So empty now, she, was no longer there.
Then the *old soldier* came to the fore,
March on he must, just as before.

I saw him going, past my door.
Just as I did, the day before.
His gait was of a man so brave.
Who with dignity, could behave.
Disappearing beyond, our street,
Who knew, what new fate, he now might meet?

George F Allen

AFTERMATH OF BOMBS

Oh, God of Wisdom, God of Truth,
How can these things remain as proof
Of Man's intent and evil ways,
The innocent with death have paid.

How can the children, pure in heart,
Be sacrificed, when they've no part,
No knowledge, of the ways of war,
Or sorrow, like an open sore.

Who are these men, what kind are they?
Do they have children, watch them play?
Have they seen pictures of our Town,
The victims, helpless, kids mown down?

Does anything stir in their hearts?
Do they know how compassion starts?
And when they close their eyes at night,
Can they still see those dreadful sights?

Did God create such men as these?
With such as them, there'll be no peace.
No place to walk, where they have been
To strike at will, create death's scene.

And families weep and Parents grieve,
As little souls depart and leave
an empty space, no-one can fill.
As evil men still maim and kill.

Joan Wheeler

FOR THOSE WHO DIED

When it was finished and the smoke had cleared, they all
sighed deeply
And swore that it shouldn't happen again
just like last time really.
And they all sat down with a list of our names and they counted
for hours
So shocked that they gave us a whole day to ourselves
So all could remember us.

Dark Dark, was the death we died for you.

So it was fine at first, clean white rows of marble gravestones
Crowds on the streets
every street and real tears too.
And little lace poppies flourished again
some bloke who'd been to Flanders after the last fight thought
of it apparently!
The show wasn't worth the price (how could it have been)
but at least they tried.

The bells tolled sad for those of us who died for you.

But the cherished faces faded in the minds of those who'd loved us
that special day of mourning turning mellow like our dust.
And the graves grew wild and the stones were scoured by wind
and rain
They sell poppies at school, paper and plastic
just to get out of lessons now.

Hard and empty was the death we died for you.

Still we're framed immortal, khaki heroes fighting brave and free
But was it brave we've asked ourselves and were we heroes?
Christ no! (and where was he when we needed him) there was
no glory
Pain, Cold, pitiful aching Death was all we savoured.

yet . . . only we ourselves recall the death we died for you.

Paul Swaffer

RETRENCHED

The slime filled trenches ran like sewage with blood soaked earth.
To drown the whispered agonies and dying cries.
Where the only light was protruding bone.
As the four horsemen of death spirited away the souls who had died

For this, I believe, was my Hell on earth.
My face a theatrical mask of blood and mud.
Distorted, by fear, into grotesque mis-shape.
But by fear and orders I to attention stood.

Then came the command, 'Over the top.'
And weary legs carried us back o'er once more.
And the sky was lit with the stab or mortar flash.
And then a score more comrades hit the floor.

Where twisted limbs, like auburn braids, intertwined.
A tangled knot of such brave humanity.
Then some half-crazed youngster raised our flag aloft.
To rationalise the impunity.

Then out of the dust and swirling smoke
A crouching figure came into sight.
With rifles raised and racing pulse.
We caught a glimpse of his rag of white.

The war was not won, but the battle was o'er.
The wounded were stretchered, to make room for more.
Rifles were cleaned, bayonets were shined.
Cigarettes were extinguished to join the dead on the floor.

Colin Knowles

BARDEEN

I had a brother
By the south-sea shore
Not by line of blood
But from the bloody line
Of duty
I was welcomed
From my Spartan cot
To his married home
We'd jape and laugh a lot
In a golden happy pause
Content
Between the politicians' wars
Parting
No time for farewell
Glass of wine or
Talk of *Auld Lang Syne*
Just *Bardeen*

Today
I asked about my brother
'Passed away,' they say
Only days before
His wife still walks this way

We meet
her face the same
beneath grey hair
A recognising smile
Warmth and sadness
We talk a little while
Until
Another lady standing nigh
Says, 'Come along my dear'
Silently we say *Bardeen*

I have a sister
By the south sea-shore.
Norman Hadland

THE BEACHHEADS

How many of those that really were there
Will feel any urge to celebrate?
Emotions that surely seared their brain,
Experiences that wracked their frame.
Such things as they will ne'er forget
Those that really were there.

They will recall, the boredom, the waiting,
The ache in the stomach, feeling of nausea,
Mind stopping tension, enveloping fear,
Pervading misery that overcame care.
Will any pleasurable memories surface
Among the thoughts of those that were there?

Sickness, the beaching, the plunge in the ocean,
Conflicting orders, chaotic confusion.
The running, the falling, the praying,
Screaming missiles, constant explosions,
Pounding heartbeat, pain of exertion.
Were the lot of those that were there.

They may see once again the face of the frightened,
The pallor, and anguish of the sorely wounded.
And as they recall the names of the fallen,
There but for the Grace of God went I
May well be the thought in many a mind,
Of the men who really were there.

S G Dollimore

BRITISH WINTERS IN WAR YEARS

We were invaded yesterday, in the night they came.
Some say those Russians are to blame.
In their thousands they dropped from the sky,
Airports disrupted, the trains cannot run.
The Government asked the Army to supply
Their lifting tackle, no use for gun.
I've attacked this menace with broom and with spade,
No other weapon has yet been made.
Sport is cancelled, many meetings close,
No post, no papers, I suppose.
The hospitals and ambulances are taking their toll.
The plight of the animals, sheep, pig and cow
When will they get fed while we are in this hole?
The police have warned everyone out on wheels,
Unless it's emergency, please stay at home.
No work for millions today, the citizen feels
As night comes again it's not time to roam.
Power and heat are in for some cuts.
The phone lines are busy, so no if's or but's.
With lorries stuck on motorways
The ports cannot help this land now.
If we still used horses, they'd get through somehow.
You've guessed it by now, I'm sure you know
I'm talking about this infernal snow . . .

Olive D Willingale

SOLDIERS 1914-18

They have grown sick far beyond their own understanding.
They have sailed too often and too far upon
The deep oceans of their great weariness.
Have looked with dull eyes and even duller hope
For something to brighten each his long night,
Have searched for and have found no star.

These men have marched a multitude of miles,
All drifting like flotsam to and fro upon the tide.
Have trudged beyond misery in mud and icy searching rain
Over the cratered ground, taking ground, losing it,
And taking it again.
Each man like Atlas, carries on his own shoulders
His fear of death and crucifying pain.

They have seen maggots feeding on the flesh of men
Who were in some other age their friends.
They have felt the jagged and hot shrapnel's breath,
Have seen it slice a man in two and seen
His warm red blood spurt out upon the mud.
A million times, each man has been a witness
To a brother soldier's death.

But they go on as if down an endless corridor
Lacking purpose, finding as they search no plan.
And each created in God's image, the pinnacle of
His creation, His great delight.
So they go like driven cattle into the shell shocked
Splinter riven night.
How long will we remember each soldier was a man?

David Tait

THE PIPES

I was crouching down in the sandy soil
trembling, in terror and fear,
for the night was full of evil sounds,
and shells were bursting near.
When through the din of battle,
on my ears there chanced to fall,
now far and faint,
now loud and near,
sounding like a clarion clear
the pipers' stirring call.
And as I gazed through that shell torn night
my eyes beheld and wondrous sight,
the men of Caledonia's might
came answering the call.
They marched in silence,
these grim faced men,
never a word they spoke,
and as they passed my heart grew calm,
and I lost my terror and fear of harm,
and my pride once more awoke,
for never a sign of fear they showed,
no hurried or trembling breath,
though they knew full well,
and I also knew,
that ere the morning's early dew
some would have met their death.
And so I rose and took my part
in that battle drear and grim,
and the hours passed on leaden feet
to a dawn that was grey and dim.
And though I watched and waited there
I waited and watched in vain
for those gallant men who had followed the pipes
would never retum again.

But their memory lives and will always live
as long as the pipes can call,
of those men who gave without a thought
for honour, and glory,
caring naught,
their love, their life, their all.

Angus Willis

JUST ANOTHER NIGHT . . .

Airframe trembling, propellers spinning,
Mighty Merlin engines dinning,
Wings straining, flexing, lifting,
Flak bursts in the sky, smoke drifting.

Pilot sweating, quietly cursing,
Gunners' eyes from turrets searching,
Target below fiercely burning,
Aircraft diving, twisting, turning.

Searchlights probing, tracer streaming,
Bombs falling, whistling, screaming
Exploding, shockwaves outward spreading,
Fighters through the mayhem threading
Guns sighting, firing, flashing,
Cannon shells flying, striking, smashing,
Electrics smoking, fuel igniting,
Crew for survival fighting.

Extinguisher working, flames are dying,
Please let this thing keep on flying!
Homeward heading, height decreasing,
Fear and tension remain unceasing.

Over the sea, nerves are twitching,
Don't much fancy the thought of ditching,
Coast in sight! Hope is growing,
Come on old girl, just keep going!

Touchdown at last, tyres screeching, smoking,
Everyone laughing, talking, joking.
Thankful not to have *got the chop.*
Just another night, another op.

W J Green

OLD COMRADES

They are going over there once more
Their promises to keep,
Pay homage to all those comrades
Who in foreign fields still sleep.

The beauty of the tended graves
The tranquil peace prevailing there
Will reassure them, dry their tears
As they offer up a silent prayer.

They will still hear the battlecries
The bullets, bombs and shells,
They will still feel the anguish,
As another comrade fell.

Old comrades they will all unite
And with hands on hearts will say,
We will remember them in the morning
And at the close of day.

So if you see the old man with medals on his chest,
Don't pass him by without a word or smile
Or a handshake of respect.

His step will be more sprightly
On his reminiscing way
He'll be proud that you remembered
What he did yesterday.

R A Clarke Ex 4th B'n KSHLI

LIBERATION AT LANGRUNE-SUR-MER 1944

Clocks stopped: For a while no more time checks.
They might be Greek, Trojan, Phoenician, Moor -
by half-light at sundown - those corroding wrecks
at sea-salty rim of this scarred shore;
but only feathered waders now slosh by, on prey intent,
where, at low water, even the sea keeps silent.

Over sunken relics creep the little waves,
implacable, primeval, timeless,
swaying mermaid tresses, sucked in sandcaves;
monsters indescribable cleave the darkness,
muzzle sand-dunes, up beaches crawling.
The inky mirror of the sea reverses all.

Immensity appals: The mind drawn out of focus,
untied, unlinked, released, perhaps to peace -
or maybe disintegrated, hurled to chaos!
Oneself stretched tenuous and alone in space,
one with the sunset, one with clouds and seacaves,
one with the silvery, creeping waves.

Behind the shore new life begins to spread.
So now from sandy beach to seaside shack return,
watched by the white gulls wheeling overhead,
and drawing curtain, lighting lamp, a poem try to earn:
Calling oneself home from swift-winged flight
across the lipped edge of darkening seas, back into light.

John Smith

BOSNIA-HERCEGOVINA

For all too long we've viewed the scenes
of shattered lives and broken dreams
Croats are suffering, there is no impunity
a war-torn zone is stripped of community

Fifty-three Croats have died over Christmas
Dubravich is shattered it's all so senseless
at early dawn the troops advance
and take position and a chance

The snow that covers camouflages
and hides the 4ft muddy trenches
and for a respite troops for warmth
will to the bunkers, what a month!

Their shifts of 24-hourly stretch
remind them of the dreadful ditch
while belching smoke from kitchen stove
feeds them beans and rice in cove

At last it's time to take a rest
fresh troops arrive they'll do their best
while weary fighters must return
to modern world devoid of fun

After 21 months of blood and chaos
there is no sign that this has paid off
the new year dawns but not for them
the cost it seems has been in vain

O would that peace begin to reign
in hearts that thought it over again
for blood that's shed for no real purpose
is innocence that cries for justice.

Lorna May Noah

BOSNIAN CHILD

Come light of day, gone dark of night
For a young child the day does start.
Bosnian born, her wretched plight
No emotion left in her heart.

No cereal for breakfast, no meat for tea
Gone the school she did attend.
Orphan of war, no family
To the fighting there is no end.

Political injustice for her kind
Confusion and poverty abounds.
Warring factions to the child are blind
Exploding mortar her daily sounds.

Dazed she wanders through the rubble
Her town has been destroyed.
Wounds made by shrapnel, the child does double
As she slips into the deep dark void.

For the child now her life is ebbing away
With no will or strength to fight.
She dies on the street in which she did play
Never knowing which side was right.

The sun is setting, gone the day
Battles are still being fought.
On the street the child starts to decay
In the crossfire other victims are caught.

The peace talks again are taking place
Will both sides this time agree?
When will the country turn around full face
Letting the children play happy and free?

Christine Johnson

DANCE. THE SARAJEVO

Ten years ago
In Sarajevo
They captured our hearts,
Gliding across the ice
To the music of Ravel.
Here was perfection,
Style,
Grace,
Beauty,
Precision.
We applauded with joy
At their ice dance

Now they skate in other cities,
But not Sarajevo.
Where people, not hearts are captured,
And bodies dance in pain
To the music of exploding shells.
And ice is stained with blood.
A performance of inhumanity
Where style is the swagger of a soldier,
No need for grace without food,
Where ugliness has deposed beauty,
Precision is the art of the sniper,
We are appalled at the misery,
Of the dance of war.

David A Garside

FALLEN WARRIOR

The dead lie strewn over the battlefield,
Romans and Celts spread across each other
in drying pools of blood. Flies circle
In the air above them like vultures.

An eerie silence pervades the plain.
The failing light of the dying sun
Casts long, dark shadows over the
Tranquil and motionless scene.

Propped up on one arm, alone
And badly wounded, a naked Celt
Lies curled on slender limbs
Amid his weapons and adornments.

Knotted muscles laced with veins
Swollen with strain ripple over
His curved back and twisted torso
Buckling beneath his weakening frame.

His head droops like a lily wilting
On its stalk and faces quietly down
His fair skin drawn taught with pain
Over facial features carved from quartz.

He breathes heavily and occasionally
Mutters incomprehensible words
Of sorrow while the life-force
Slowly seeps from his wounds.

He can see the faces of his family
Reflected in the cool, green grass
Of his homeland and hear old tales
Told in whispers gently on the wind.

Stan Morton

REQUIEM FOR HMS GLORIOUS

The chaos of the Norwegian campaign
Has scattered the carrier's squadrons.
The Tide of War has swept us,
Lock, stock and gun-barrel,
Onto this Lincolnshire shore.
While all Hell breaks loose at Dunkirk,
Bees, not bullets, wing their purposeful way
Between the camouflaged hangars,
Seeking only the rich red clover.
The scene is one of tranquillity -
Only the rabbits are fearful
As they crouch in the lush pasture,
Criss-crossed by the wheel tracks of landing aircraft.

Twelve Fairey Swordfish,
Accustomed to a flight deck in constant motion,
Brood in the lone dispersal;
Their wings folded (shipboard fashion)
And wheels chocked fore and aft on unfamiliar turf.
They face a salt breeze, fresh off the Jutland Bank,
Which pipes a long lament
In their struts and wires,
Commiserating with them in their orphaned state -
In the loss of their ship,
And those who shared her fate
In waters north of the Arctic Circle.

It is haymaking time,
The air is sweet with the sounds and scents of summer
(And the voice of Judy Garland singing *Over the Rainbow).*
While we are grateful for our good fortune
And thankful that so many have returned from Dunkirk;
Though we have been honoured with visits from the King,
And Winston Churchill -
We feel little joy,
Because of the fifteen hundred shipmates who perished,
And in whose comradely memory
We close ranks for the forthcoming battle.

Bill Clayton

THE LISTS

In memory of those Twenty Three St Columba's College, Co Dublin, First XI cricketers who died on active service in the two World Wars

The rain beats down: Pavilion-shelter gained,
Both teams pace to and fro, in anxious mood,
Impatient to resume, like tigers chained.
Silent, through sensing I should not intrude,
I face our bygone teams on wooden panels,
Since 1857 in our annals.

The rain beats down: Hardened, I've turned my back
Upon the gloomy sight of flooded ground,
Scanning those names, immortalised in black,
Which here, year after year, in lists abound:
When current voices, querulous, accost
My ears with *dreadful tragedy . . . points lost . . .*

Lost . . . tragedy . . . this triggers off the thought
Of marble lists the Chapel walls contain,
Part-duplicated on these walls. Distraught,
My mind now switches to those fields of pain
Where Twenty Three of these, to no applause,
Laid down their lives to serve a Righteous Cause.

These, who had played at College Park, Rathmines,
Woodbrook, Rathfarnham, Wicklow, Greystones, Kells,
Were slaughtered in the foremost fighting lines:
The Somme, Ypres, Passchendaele, The Dardanelles.
But here, above that field where they once played,
Their names remain, on Cricketing Parade:-

De Rinzy, Brennan, Shaw, Smyth, Neale, Read, Scott,
Hone, Finlay, Patterson, Webb, Crookshank, Eagar,
On foreign fields were gassed, dismembered, shot,
Like *Hinds, Jones, Beatty, Hill.* Their prize a meagre
Memorial in chiselled stone, as gratitude,
Since deep-felt loss finds refuge in a platitude.

The rain beats down: Play cannot be resumed.
Resumed . . . along the lists I sadly glance:-
Knox-Perkins, Griffith, Martin, Northridge - doomed.
McClintock (Burma), *H E Oswald* (France).
All Twenty Three in St Columba's Annals
Appearing both in Khaki and in Flannels.

Abandoned! Now the players trudge away,
Cursing the bitter blows of hostile fate . . .
But all will live to fight another day,
Unlike the Twenty Three. I contemplate
Their two memorials. Placed here, among
Their fellow cricketers, they live, still young.

Morgan Dockrell

REQUIEM FOR A BROTHER

F/Lt Lennert Axel Komaroff, RAF

You took your last flight
in the navigator's seat
of a plane produced in wood -
aptly named *Mosquito.*

I can hear the buzz in the night sky
on that last foray over Arnhem:

I can see the sea of white crosses
still tended by Dutch friends
at Bergen-op-Zoom, where you
now rest-in-peace.

At best, in London, I can attend
the placings of small wooden crosses
and poppies annually in the gardens
of Westminster Abbey on Remembrance Day.

Today, some fifty years later,
I remember that afternoon siesta
following a Sunday *tiffin,* when
you and I banged each other with pillows -
feathers flying inside our Mosquito house -
a mesh-wire cage within the nursery
for protection.

And *Olo* Amah rushing in, throwing
Wide open the protective entry, calling

'Rest time. Rest time. No makee
noise. Mummy, Daddy sleep.'

That night in Shanghai, our young bodies
were covered in bites.
Amah had given the waiting enemy
the opportunity to fly in.

Sadly, Lenny, you were not so lucky
over Arnhem, being spotted
and swatted by gunfire!

But we do not forget
and wish you were still here
Son of a Mosquito!

Arda Lacey

PEGASUS BRIDGE

Dedicated to Major John Howard MC and the men of the 2nd Battalion, Oxfordshire and Buckinghamshire Light Infantry.

By air to battle
Borne on silent wings,
Gambling against the odds
That is the nature of things.

Deathly pale in the east,
Stirs the anxious dawn
Whilst to the west
Lies the hostile Orne.

'Twixt Canal and River
Our Drop-Zone lay,
Chosen to be the first
For this historic day.

Release the tow,
Nose down, rudder right.
Horsas, black shadows
Slip noiseless through the night.

Ahead the bridge
We are the key
To open Fortress Europe
Just us, Gliders three.

Swishing lower, centre stick,
The wire, the trenches,
Give the rudder a kick
Now slam her down.

The Major's out
With Chamberlain behind
Hugging the ground
Some cover to find.

Mortars and grenades,
Shatter the night
Well entrenched, the enemy
Put up a stiff fight.

The Ox and Bucks,
A bare ninety strong,
Sweep over the bridge
Which seems five miles long.

Securing each end
And the *Gondree* home,
They dig in and wait
For the Commandos to come.

The pipes of Bill Millin
Proclaim the battle is won,
John Howard and his Troop
Know their job is done.

Lord Lovat apologises
'Sorry, you had to wait,
We were due here at twelve,
'Fraid we're two minutes late.'

Lt Col Dennis Hampton Jeffery

COMRADESHIP

Fear marched beside him
dragging his feet
And, in a cruel embrace,
whispered, *retreat!*
But Comradeship took
the soldier's hand,
Left, right, left, across
a foreign land,
As he kept up with the column.

Later, huddled close in
the evening chill,
With the world at war now
silent and still,
For a timeless few hours
his heart felt peace
And he wished the moment
would never cease;
By dawn he was ready with the column.

His body ached with cold,
right to the bone,
Whilst his mind escaped
to the hills of home;
Fishing for trout with a
spinner or two,
An oakwood, a cornfield,
a fine English view,
As he trudged in the wake of the column.

In time the soldier became
a comrade,
Found strength in unity when
his courage strayed;
He learned about valour and
facing the foe,
To endure bravely when his
spirit was low
And how to march step by step with the column.

Rose Savage

ARMISTICE

Once again it is Armistice Day
And sad thoughts fill the mind
Recalling names and faces
Of the comrades we left behind
Remembering youthful well trained men
Of when their spirits were high
How bravely they were to acquit themselves
Now in foreign fields they lie

That embracing feeling of *Esprit-de-Corps*
And the camaraderie
Friendships that were forever forged
On the anvil of history
Determined rugged faces
Men on whom you could rely
Unknowing as yet their destiny
To live, or perhaps to die

I remember them with affection
Those daring, gallant soldiers
With Guardsman's bearing and historic pride
Set squarely upon their shoulders
The honour of the regiment
Was something they held dear
And safely they held it in their hands
Never once to disappear

So every year I journey
To the hall of memory
For me it's become a pilgrimage
For they feel so close to me
A feeling almost of solitude
Though surrounded by a throng
Abide With Me we chorus
That sad and mournful song

It never fails to move me
And tears come into my eyes
Moments of emotion
That I cannot disguise
I find my shoulders straightening
And my thoughts become benign
In memory, I touch them
And a shiver runs down my spine

And when the bugler plays *Last Post*
The most poignant moment for me
That final mournful tribute
Stirring the memory
So let us never forget them
And the ultimate price they paid
We raise our hand in a final salute
Rest In Peace - old Comrades.

J Newman

FIFTY YEARS LATER

The date was June Nineteen Forty Four
We couldn't let Hitler win the war -
Our brave young lads in khaki and blues
Knew that the time had come to choose
Between the jackboot and repression
Or peace on earth and free expression.
At last the dawn of the D-Day landing
The fight before them tough and demanding.
They stuck to the task with true British heart
Till the last of the Nazis were seen to depart
But not without a very high price -
Some paid with the ultimate sacrifice.
It's fifty years since the Flanders flowers
Were stained with their blood for this land of ours
And the peace we've enjoyed across those years
Was bought with their blood and sweat and tears.
So let their grandchildren join in the fun
To commemorate what they had done
Those lads would not want us still to be sad,
But enjoy the life they made sure we had.
We will always remember with thanks and pride
The horror, the wounded and those who died,
Their courage and sacrifice won't be in vain
So long as man's love for his Country remain.

D N Wright

NORMANDY

Gale force winds have turned to heat
And dust lies on the ground
Any movement stirs it up
And death falls all around

Sudden terror grips us all
We hear the dreaded clanks
Every soldier fears the worst
When faced with Tiger tanks

Moaning Minnies sear the mind
Quite different from all others
Soldiers hug the earth in fear
Some shout for their mothers

The teller and the *S* mines
Are meant to kill or maim
They take away your manhood
And leave a broken frame

The shot, the shell, the mortar
The carnage and the screams
Will live with us for evermore
And haunt us in our dreams

Sat beside a flowing stream
My head held in my hand
I dream the dreams of yesterday
In a free, untroubled land

The battlefield is silent now
The guns have gone to sleep
While Pioneers collect the dead
And stack them in a heap

Roy Bennett

TRENCH WARFARE

Sent to no-man's land
Troopship Penned
For who knows what?
And who knows why?
Young innocent lambs
Trapped in a nightmare fold
On a field called Armageddon.

Plunged into the cold and wet
Of an earthy dug out home
Where there's bully beef, and Rosie-Lee
If a stomach's fit to take it
They had to forge a cold steel mind
And their truest friend they were to find
Was that bayoneted rifle!

Frightened faces drained of colour
Cork dry mouths, and knotted gut
Of those huddled youthful warriors
Waiting nerve wracked for the signal
Of the count down Captain's Whistle
Duty bound, they daren't resist -
It's over the top and Nemesis!

The Hun's machine gun in its nest
A deadly staccato sings
And shells that whistle overhead
Blast level earth to moonscape
With grim craters and canals
Filled with tangled, mangled bodies
Of the ones who didn't make it.

In the awful stony silence
When the battle took its rest
Nothing better than the comfort
Of a soothing cigarette
And the needful gritty humour
Bonding comrades close together -
Helped to bind the crumbling brickwork of the mind.

A little ground was slowly won
But what a price to pay
Young Innocence had quickly gone -
From boys to men in a day
They thought about tomorrow's world
While the sad white dove looked down -
Black with disappointment.

Don Atherton

A NEW TOMORROW

O'er there across the angry sea
Of this we have no doubt.
Those gallant men of liberty
Their lonely souls cry out.
Listening to the voices argue
Power and glory
Whilst battle scarred and weary men
Are left to tell the story.
They carry on regardless
No matter what the cost
No matter how the heartache burns
When precious lives are lost.
We remember them with pride
Their dignity, they reserve,
Honouring crown and country
And regiment which they serve.
To those who lose their loved ones
What can we do, what can we say
Who will bear their sorrow
At the dawn of each new day.
Someone's loved one, someone's brother, someone's
Buddy, someone's son has suffered
The treachery of the bullet and the bomb.

We must let the voice of freedom
Sound with a mighty roar
To put our hearts and minds at ease
Then peace will reign once more
In a land fit for heroes to live
Filled with duty, love and pride
We will welcome a new tomorrow
With loved ones by our side.

Rosemary Chatterton

ON THE HOME FRONT, AND THE END OF WORLD WAR II

We were tired of ration books, gas masks in boxes
wail of the sirens to warn of air raids,
then hurrying to shelters, but mostly at night
for work cannot stop, this war must be won.
The factories hum with machinery and chat,
as the workers try hard to reach their target.
The quota gets higher, there's pride to achieve.
The fire-fighters and wardens are glad of a rest
after working all night, putting out fires;
or rescuing people, trapped in houses in piles
of rubble and dust. It's morning, raid's over -
people pour from the underground, where they've slept,
and go home for a wash and change of their clothes.
After breakfast - it's off to offices, shops
or wherever they work, another day started.
Nurses and doctors work night and day
on those wounded by bombs or dragged from wreckage
of homes or shelters - no longer existing;
while the dead are removed, and identified later
by sorrowing families, desolate, bereft.
Kind hands and voices try hard to comfort
bereaved and homeless, volunteers hurry
to offer a refuge, food, clothes or a bed.
The war gets worse, with devilish devices
sent by our enemies - rockets and buzz bombs.
Grim and determined as we fight back
for our freedoms, our loved ones, all we hold dear.
Comes the end of the war, last *all clear* sounding,
bells peal joyously, we dance and we shout.
There's hugging and kissing, war is over at last -
Hitler defeated, but, oh what a price -
Thousands lie dead, or wounded and shocked
in hospital wards, or they languish at home.
Let us hope for peace that is worldwide, and long lasting.

V Graver

THE WAR TO FIND

It has been said that there is a time for all things.
But what of war?
And what of peace?
And when is the time for reconciliation?
Can there be peace in the sound of a trumpet,
or war within the bosom of silence?
Yes, these things (and more) are possible,
as life is but an expression of man's inner self;
From where happiness and contentment can surely evolve,
and grow into that which is more beautiful
than man's shadow of himself:
Afraid not of sunlight, or the zest of life.
Inert, but projected
to the seen and the unseen:
Harmonious intercourse of the throbbing life blood
of the Universal Spirit,
in which no cancer exists.
Purity of souls.
The essence of being, in perfect harmony.
Oh - how can this be?
It is, and always was, and always will be:
Through love it is there for all to discover.
The charity of God.
Go forward into immortality without fear
fighting the battle for inner peace.

Ivan Sanders

BELLIGERENT FOOD

Breakfast is eaten, thirty two kids, thirteen mothers, some eggs, milk and not a slice of feelings.

Lunch is an easy picking, grandparents on sticks popped in a scoop, a burp and the bullet heads giggle.

Evenings have a cocktail of innocent blood cells split, spitting lust on vestal woman.

Mark Cachia

AT DAWN ABOARD A TROOPSHIP

The sky is grey
And beneath my feet the ship moves,
Gently giving way to the swell of the ocean.
Dawn is near. The sky lightens in the east,
At first a golden glow and then a reddish arc appears.
The expanse of limitless sea becomes less harsh
As if warmed by the sunrise,
The coldness of the morning becomes less chilly,
The wavecaps begin to gleam.
Day has begun in this vastness of space.
It is a long way from Singapore to Aden.
Tomorrow will be the same
And the day after.
I sigh, knowing not why
And go below.

Stan Ward

A CHILD AT WAR

A drooping smile upon his face
And dark hair slipping over his careless eyes,
He trod the barely familiar stair,
In old trousers and no shoes or socks
With teddy tumbling on behind.
He had come to Granny in the country
Escaping London in the war.
Bombs and Nazis had had no effect
On his cheerily smiling countenance
And bayonets and grenades were words
As confusing and unknown as many others.
He saw his mother at the table
With Sister and Granny keen in silent comfort.
He glimpsed the yellowy paper in her pale hands
And the salt upon her cheeks and nose
Before his sister came out to him
To hurry him up the stairs.
In his foolhardy innocence he never realised
That he would never again see
The tall man, as dark as he was,
Home on leave for a few days.
The man he once called: *Daddy.*

Jane Watson

WORLD AT WAR

World at war what is our plight,
Wounding and killing all through the night.

Daybreak brings total devastation,
Homes and lives have been wrecked,
Through meaningless liaisons.

Give a thought to our children,
They are our future,
What standards we set,
To maim and butcher.

Shirley Porter

GULF WAR '91

Dressed in their uniforms
Military hats on young heads.
Because of the Gulf War
Young lives now dead.
Their young faces
On an English newspaper page
Proves war is plainly an outrage.

Bernadette O'Reilly

WAR ZONE

Death came swiftly that winter's day
Encased in shells of silvered steel
Earth, snow and ice formed bleak grey shrouds
For the young bodies once at play
She saw explosions ending life
Weeping she cradled her dying son
Ten years old, her spirit's joy
Shattered by hate and bitter strife
They laid him to rest in a frozen field
Near the ruined church where they prayed
A plain wooden cross now bears his name
With the date when his fate was sealed
She yearns each day for lasting peace
Tolerance, love and the will to forgive
To feel safe, to live without fear
For the ache in her heart to cease.

Ida Whitfield

CRY OUT YOUR BATTLECRY!

Cry out your battlecries today;
Yes glory if you may!
For victory in blood was cost;
And sanities were lost!

You taught your children how to kill;
You taught them it with skill!
But could you please just answer this;
How many must you kill?

On every page, on every screen,
A view of war unclean;
Is painted oh so vividly,
Yet only glory's seen.

Yes plastic guns are in their hands
In all the distant lands;
And war is seen but as a game -
Where there's no dead or lame.

P A Imbriani

ALL OVER AGAIN

Why do all the poppies blow
when the soldiers sing their hymns
and all the prayers are spoken,
they died to save their country
they died to save the world
do you think that they would be happy
to know that it's happening all over again.

So the songs are sung
and the dead remembered
all are wrapped in glory
and so the celebrations end,
but the glorious inhumanity
and the cruelty shown to fellow men
as those that we remember
are surely not blame free.

Where are the words of reason
that would condemn this insanity
to pages in our history books,
will not one voice sing out the message
dear God what have we done
for it is happening all over again.

Ian Ambrose

WAR

Sadness is a lonely heart,
Bereft by war and torn apart,
Away from home and family,
To drift along so aimlessly.

Devastation in this land,
No-one to lend a helping hand,
No water food or welcome light
Only darkness and endless night.

Fighting, dying, where will it end
No smiling face, no-one a friend
Will help be coming, maybe too late,
What of life, what is our fate.

Exhausted my head begins to spin,
No sign of hope I feel within.
Just a numbness cold and raw,
Why must we fight this senseless war.

Edna Walford Harvey

THE TIDE OF WAR

I stood at the edge of a yawning crevasse,
And gazed at the scene far below -
(Two mighty nations stood facing in line)
And wondered which way they would go.

They stood there uneasy, their armours amassed,
The soldiers they shout and they jeer.
(Their leaders were safe as they talked far away)
And the nations just waited in fear.

And then, as I watched, the signal was given
(One soldier had just fired his gun)
The armies they fought and the guns they all roared -
The war to end wars had begun.

The bodies piled up as the killing went on
And slowly, far in the West,
A red tide arose and engulfed all below -
The young of the nations, the best.

I stood on the edge of the yawning crevasse
And watched the red tide of the war
(I knew that the leaders were safe in their homes)
But the soldiers were living no more.

Alison J White

INDIAN CAVALRY - HAIL AND FAREWELL

They are gone, gone for ever, the days I remember
When proudly I rode at the Regiment's head,
Sikhs, Jats and Punjabis, the *Bengal Rissala,*
Let's drink to the Old Days, the days that are dead.
The Farewell Parade, when our well beloved horses,
Bays, Browns and Chestnuts, the Regiment's pride,
For the last time were part of His Majesty's Forces,
Then we were dismounted, with nothing to ride.
But the Men were still there, and as ducks take to water
They took to their new mounts, light tank, armoured car,
As their fathers before them across the Black Water
They sailed to do battle for King and Sirkar.
Battle dress and black beret replaced the gay splendour
Of scarlet and silver, dark blue and gold,
With Bren gun and Mortar they fought just as stoutly
As fought their forefathers, the Lancers of old.
Drink to the men of the old Bengal Lancers,
Drink the Cavalry Spirit that still
Burns in the hearts of Sikh, Jat and Punjabi.
As it did in our day and, Please God, always will.

Lt Col R A A Dawes MC

GALLIPOLI

His letters told of love; his hopes were high
That he'd return to find a brighter day.
He had no thought or fear that he would die.

The chaos on the beach, the smoking sky
Were tests of his resolve; it did not sway.
His letters told of love; his hopes were high.

Though comrades fell, and opened wide the lie
That *Dulce et decorum . . .* showed the way,
He had no thought or fear that he would die.

And through it all he knew he must deny
The awful truth, so those at home could say
'His letters told of love; his hopes were high.'

His mind withdrew, could not afford to sigh
For bodies left to fester and decay.
He had no thought or fear that he would die.

And when he saw the bullets pass him by
He felt he was immune, kept death at bay.
His letters told of love; his hopes were high -
He had no thought or fear that he would die.

John Tickner

BOMB INCIDENT REMEMBERED
ST MICHAEL PATERNOSTER ROYAL, LONDON, 1944

Dust returning and crimson striped
Circles round the cavernous hole
Of a thrice mayoral crypt
Resting on a flying soul.
No bells from the stricken city
Called out the spirit of the past
Stirred a moving aching pity
To return again at last.
That presence stayed with me beyond
In touch with my sight and feeling,
A flying bomb; a ghostly bond
Are London bells now pealing?
I saw or felt this church's grave
Reaching to us beneath the wave.

Alan Dickson

FIVE YEARS

Written in the Autumn of 1944, when the Eighth Army was building up astride Route 16, on the East coast of Italy.

Do you remember how, five years ago,
We walked the lane at noon, and laughed, and planned
The world? For then the War was young -the sand
Unstirred in Africa. We did not know
What lay in store for us - how France would go
Into the night, a lost, bewildered land,
Leaving to us alone the hopeless stand,
While John would die amid the Norway snow.

Five years ago! The years, the miles, are far
Between that lane and this long Southern street
Where we are massed to march, to deal the blow
That shall avenge the years. A desert star
Is ours to wear, who did Defeat.
We go - and John goes with us as we go!

F K Forrester

UNTITLED

Guerrilla warfare
is a military technique
not a political action.
Individual attacks,
surprise raids by small groups,
the evasion of pitched battle
is well suited to revolutionary action.
It is pre-eminently
the instrument of
the war of liberation.

Fred Brown

SPACE VOYAGER

They named it for the War God, long ago
When stars were living beings of the sky.
Red planet, shining through the evening dusk,
Its hue seen clearly by the naked eye,
And yet - maybe our fathers got it wrong.
The fair blue planet Earth is torn with strife.
Across the continents small wars abound.
We watch our screens, the daily loss of life
And shattered cities gaping to the sky
With spreading deserts, ruin creeping more
Across our Earth as man fights brother man.
Perhaps this planet should be named for war.
A film brought Martian landscape into view
And made one wonder. Have we been there, too?

Audrey Forbes-Handley

PEACE

People always fighting,
People being shot
Whilst the people in the middle
Dream of the peace they haven't got.
Helpless little children,
Their families and their friends
Living through the war
That never seems to end.
Peace would mean freedom -
Everyone loving and caring;
Nobody being selfish -
Everybody giving and sharing.
Peace would bring justice -
The world could unite,
Peace would bring an end
To the war and the fight.

Lucy Symington

NOTHING LIKE

There's nothing like the stare
of concentration camp despair,
skin hangs in folds
over bones grown old.

Nothing like the gape
of a victim of rape,
drunken soldier's amusement
is her bemusement.

Nothing like the surprise
in a dead child's eyes,
his game interrupted,
family disrupted.

Nothing like the cold
of the dispossessed old,
homes burned and pillaged
in peaceful village.

Nothing like.

Mary Blake

D-DAY

On the 6th of June 1944
Britain could plainly see,
That every man must play their part,
In order to be free.

Men filled boats of every kind,
Set off - on *'OK let's go'*
Determination overcame their fear
As they went to conquer their foe.

Bravely, the gliders went overhead,
And sealed the enemy behind,
And pushed them forward, into the sailors' hands
The Germans knew they had been blind.

We may wonder why they risked so much
For many of the bold men died,
But it was because they loved their country
And they knew God was on their side.

Grace Herron (13)

NO PEACE

Wreaths around the Cenotaph,
Poppies sold red for blood
To remind us of our brave and valiant men
Who died in fields of mud.
But can we who had no part in war
Really imagine the suffering and pain,
Will remembrance make certain
It will not happen again.
I don't think it ever will,
Look at Ireland day after day,
Look at Bosnia's suffering
It doesn't go away.
While guns are held in human hands,
While greed eats someone's soul,
And while some countries can't defend themselves
War will play its role.
Until we love one another
And really care about a world as one
Then guns will blaze and people will die
And nobody can ever say they've won.

J M Jones

THEIR LONGEST DAY

Resting quietly from the violence
raging on that foreign shore
soldier, sailor, airman sleeping
broken by a savage war

Bravely had they died those heroes
men who crossed those special lines
bereft of feeling, sight and hearing
scarred by bullets, steel and mines

The bittersweet of bloody battle
fraught with dangers, fear and hate
scathed with misery and pain
their death a travesty of fate

Midst this pantomime of carnage
fatal wounds that never heal
a mask where once there smiled a face
shows now an agony that's real

What price this victory they won
how then to count the cost
a solitary cross of wood
to mark each tragic life that's lost.

John E Barnard

WHY DO MEN HAVE TO DIE

If men have to fight a war
Why do they have to die.
Can't politicians find a way
To stop the tears and sighs.

If men have to go to fight
And leave behind their wives,
Can't they try to find a way
To come home with their lives.

If men have to fight a war
Why can't they all come home,
Not die and lay in some foreign field
Just a name upon a stone.

If men are sent to fight a war
Under some distant sky,
What's the point of winning
If no-one understands why.

Maggie Bradley

BACK IN WORLD WAR TWO

Back in World War Two the skies
Were full of giant metal flies,
Twirling twisting, diving, turning,
The fuel in their engines really burning.

Back in World War Two it seemed
The thing that every boy had dreamed,
Machine guns blazing - a terrific sound,
Sending enemies to the ground.

Back in World War Two the booms
From the bombs shook all the rooms,
Planes flying through the cold night air,
Blasting Germans here and there.

Back in World War Two the shout,
As came at night the big blackout,
And like a made rush for a helter-skelter,
People dashed straight to the shelter.

Back in World War Two did they die,
Maybe shot or bombed - but why?
Did a nation do this? I don't know, do you?
That was all back in World War Two.

Dominic Mulreany

LAST DUTY

They fold the flag, impersonal hands
drawing corner to corner, drawing down
your blind. Your coffin stands, stark
and polished, surrounded by flowers.
For you now, dark is deeper
than night under alien skies,
towering black. To moum
is our solace. Your sleep dies content;
you did the right that forced you
to its duty. Dawn of manhood
called your country's summons,
and you went. We think of all
you could have been, surrendered
for your peace, and peace for humankind.
Our pride is yours; your pride is total.

Alison Chisholm

EMBARKATION LEAVE, 1944

Back from the strong and tireless arms
Of wife and children, now must go
The soldier sworn to victory;
He feels awhile their love and warms
His heart, which soon must overflow
With tears that none could ever see.

In these bright, scurrying days he felt
A peace unsullied by the strife -
Forgotten are those marching feet -
And here the unfettered spirit dwelt
To learn again the art of life,
In war's surcease, a bitter sweet.

Now to the fight where nations fall
Headlong across the eastern sea,
The warrior goes without a name;
Hears in the distance many a call
Sent from a global threnody
And answering sails, with the world aflame.

Randle Manwaring

YOU'LL NEVER WALK ALONE

In memory of Tom Price,
born 1 September 1919, died 9 December 1993

Another old soldier died today
No cut flowers for me, he'd tell
He long ago escaped the fray
So songs for him, as they toll the bell.

Another old soldier died today
He fought the good fight as I heard tell
No medals now can he display
On tunic bright, as they toll the knell.

Another old soldier died today
Our good friend Tommy, I heard tell
No longer pain he'll bear you'll say
But Poppy Wreath, with those that fell.

Another old soldier died today
No more for him a place in the sun
But he's still *Singing In The Rain*
The final note from him . . . *Have Fun.*

Enid Ashton

REMEMBRANCE

The old war veterans' Cenotaph eyes brimmed
With tears as he recalled his fallen
Comrades in arms:
So many fathers, brothers, and sons.
Some of them, he had known very well.
Good mates - pals he had grown up with all
Through his childhood and school days.
Others, he knew not at all.
But, all of them had fought and died for the
Same, common cause:-
Freedom.

The wreath in his heart again felt the sharp,
Bitter pain of loss of his dear friends and
Fellow Britons.
One half of his soul thanked God for sparing his life.
The other half wished he had died with them.
But, in his heart, he knew that he had survived
Those long-gone dark days for a very special reason:
And, that reason was to never forget them,
And remember them.
Always.

R E Sharp

NORMANDY . . . 1944 AND ALL THAT

In Normandy I died a little - a German soldier wrote,
we all knew what he meant when we got off the boat;
those dead cows in the meadows among the grass so green;
all farmers would have die a bit had they those pastures seen.

Civilians, more than a bit crazed, in between battle caught;
each village and farmhouse of boobytrap and sniper fraught;
twenty-five pounders blasting, answered by an eighty-eight;
Jerries' mortars so accurate they could hit a dinner-plate.

In Normandy I died a bit - the German soldier said,
from Bayeux up to Caen some were already dead;
bayoneted rifle inverted in the ground with helmet on the top
the story of a comrade to mates who must not stop.

Cheux, Caumont, Villers Bocage, up to Carpiquet
there was no harvesting of corn or saving of the hay;
it was *Tank Commander . . . Tank Commander . . . Come blow your horn,*
there's Tigers in the hull down and spandaus in the corn.

Oh the yellow corn was trampled . . . in places it was black
where a tank had brewed up . . . *Look how it shed its track.*
The farmhouse has no roof, you note in search for wine;
Old Smudger's got a leg wound . . . isn't he a lucky swine?

When going out on patrol all remove their pack,
Watch our for Jerry going forward . . . our blokes coming back,
In that ditch there in the meadow is there sniper or platoon?
Keep your ruddy head down or you'll find out all too soon.

In Normandy I died a little, the German soldier said,
thank God we should both he and me, we are not completely dead,
we'll think of European unity . . . and though problems there will be,
it will be better than '44 in Normandy . . . I'm sure Jerry would agree.

Lewis Rowe

THE LAST WATCH

A hazy distant coastline,
Slips silently from sight.
The only sound the bow waves hiss,
As day fades into night.

Diamond bright the stars sprawl,
Across the ink black dome.
Closed up at action stations,
The men tell tales of home.

Tense and watchful faces
Hide their thoughts and fears.
Ready at a moment's notice,
For action beyond their years.

How many will see the dawn break
And the sun in the eastern sky?
How many will breath the morning air
And hear the sea birds cry?

How many will see tomorrow . . .

Howard Atkinson

OUR FRIENDS LIE THERE

Our friends lie there beneath the
sweet green turf of Normandy. They
sleep, row on row as they have slept
for fifty years. We left them there
when we came home from war.

The children place their flowers
beside each small white stone. Innocent
tokens of their gratitude to soldiers
of the second war, who crossed the sea
to die for freedom's sake.

And we old men, veterans of that time
so long ago, when young men died to give
us lives of peace, return to pay our
homage, shed our tears, and hear their
voices in our dreams. They were our
friends, and we salute them, as they
lie sleeping there.

Brian Gregan

MEANING OF D-DAY

The day of devastation .
Fifty years ago
The day of destination
When only play was left to show
The day of decision
Of sadness and sorrow
The day of all days
For 37,000 there will be no tomorrow
Bodies torn in the wreckage
Shadows of heroes past
Each doing their best
Praying that today, would not be their last
One day in June
Such a great loss of lives
All that grief at home
For mothers, loved ones and wives,
A day of destruction
For so many men
Tales from D-Day veterans
Who painfully recall it, yet again.

Lawrence A McGranaghan

CHRISTMAS IN WAR TIME

Today, new meanings grow immense
Yet bring the heart a store
Of blessings, a rare confidence
And quiet at the core.

Endless distractions which once scratched
The surface of the mind,
Are vanquished; anger's gate is latched,
We have no axe to grind.

Where in the brain they wantoned free,
Those doubts which come from our
Confusion and duality,
They bow to this Babe's power.

Faith antidoting fear of doom,
However perilous
Our state, we bless this maid through whom
Grace is returned to us.

Across the terminals of fear
Love like a sudden spark
Has leaped, and in this Infant here
Light has replaced the dark!

H O Brian O'Neil

LITTLE BOY SOLDIER

It's a happy day, the sun shines bright
A new baby boy held under the light
The mother smiles, the father gleams
The little boy cries, it's not what it seems

Then one day the boy grows up
He hits his teens, they fill his cup
The boy is trained and disciplined
He jumps to his feet upon command

Now the boys blood is free and flowing
His eyes - they slowly close
The blood, the dirt, the tears, the scars.
Little boy soldiers get sent home in jars.

Amen.

Anya Nyx

SOLDIERS' FAREWELL

What thoughts in my heart do anguish
as I rest my weary head upon my shoulder
So much suffering I can bear no more
my love for you dearest is deeper than the deepest seas
And warmer than the Sahara
Oh what grief lies within my heart
all stresses and trials it seems
Until I think of you
then all at once my thoughts set aglow
like the hot kindles of fire
that glow in exultation.
Has thou not given me power
to overcome these tribulations
And rejoice in all the joys of happiness
Give me one wish at least
to end my life in Peace.

Pamela Harrison

MARCHING TUNE

Setting off, pipes playing, kilts swinging,
Our company moved at ease, grand, proud.
Who are you going to meet, Jock?
Watch your bloody feet, Jock.
As we marched along the old Crieff Road.

Colin McIntyre

RANVILLE

I stood alone amidst a crowd
With tear-dimmed eyes, head slightly bowed.
Then, from afar, there came a sound
As from a phantom battle-ground.
With straining ears, I heard a call
And to the ground I saw him fall
With body limp and painful eyes.
Is this the way a soldier dies?
Then through the mist, across the dune,
There came an old familiar tune;
A bugle call from ages past
But when I raised my eyes at last
A field of crosses came in sight
Of men who fought for what was right.
I saw vague figures standing there,
Heads held down, they stood in prayer.
My eyes were drawn towards a grave.
It was my friend I could not save.

Cyril Crain

THE CONSCIENTIOUS OBJECTOR

My soul is torn this way and that,
No-one's more loyal than I,
But kill my fellow man I can't
I will not make him die.

The war envelopes all our lives,
My duty it should be
To join the forces of the King
In air, on land or sea.

My family and friends look down
On me with searing scorn,
But wiping out the sons of God
'Twas not for this we're born.

If I am let I'll do my bit,
I'll work until I drop,
But slay my fellow man I'll not,
Just pray for war to stop.

R M Norton

REMEMBRANCE SUNDAY

Each dying year, when the Armistice parade
Snaps a smart *eyes right* to the stiff-stood Mayor,
I note the shrinking numbers who assemble there,
Behind the willing bugles of the Boys' Brigade.

And I remember her who shed secret tears
When that foul obscenity, the First World War,
Silenced a well-loved voice for evermore,
Right at the end of those four fateful years.

Her unrequited love was multiplied
By later generations, who went away
To be maimed and mutilated, and who died
In untold thousands every day.

That is why, when this day comes round, early each November,
It is they who waited 'til they could wait no more that I remember.

Dan Pugh

THE WAR TO END WAR 1914 - 1918

Now let the wild drums rattle and the women weep
Slow tears of sorrow for the eyeless dead:
Wrapped in the blind contentment of eternal sleep
They'll seek no reckoning for the blood they shed.

But when the drums are silent and the trumpets sing
High songs of victory in a wasted world
Then shall their fame in every farthest corner ring,
Their name enduring though their flags be furled.

Then in the heart of London's city will we raise
Like an accusing finger, pointing lies,
A fair white monument of chiselled stone, in praise
Of those who died, to save and make us wise,

To which, in later years, the sons of light
Shall lift their eyes as they go forth - to fight.

Peter Fenwick

DEDICATED TO THE BATTLE OF BRITAIN AIRMEN

The foe came over here in their countless hordes
To bomb and blast this island of the free.
To save this fair land from democracy
At the behest of tyrannous warlords.

Our men rose up to meet them in the sky,
And made the battle field away up there.
They shot, and blew, and swept them from the air,
For Britain, freedom's champion dare not die.

The foe returned again to the attack,
By night and day, in cloud, in rain, and sun,
But our men kept watch for every murd'ring Hun,
And shot them down, or sent them fleeing back.

The debt we owe to our brave men can never be repaid
For they wrote the finest chapter in Britain's history
And they have covered themselves in everlasting glory
In doing their best, by the sacrifices they made.

Wilf Farries

THE YOUNG SOLDIER

With frightened eyes he looked around,
At comrades - dead upon the ground.
From eager throats had come the cry,
Kill or be killed - conquer or die.

They'd marched out like men with a target in view,
The right of their cause had carried them through.
They'd all fought like fiends through those hours of hell,
Through blasting of bomb - and whining of shell.

Like a man he had fought - with courage and joy.
But stood now, a terrified shivering boy.
The air filled with silence, the fighting was done,
Though his comrades he'd lost, the battle was won.

The groans of the dying, the smell of the dead,
Brought tears to his eyes, and a heart full of dread,
And his stomach heaved at this terrible sight,
For he was just a boy, and too young to fight.

Gone was the Glory, his heart filled with pain.
As he wept for the friends that he'd not see again.
With a mind growing old, this youngster now saw,
The sadness, stupidity, cruelty of war.

Dorothie E Stalton

THE SEARCHING SOLDIER

I found him,
Kneeling on one knee,
With head bowed,
Away from me,
As if the weariness,
Had overtaken him.
As if the horror,
And the frustration,
Had brought submission,
To this young man,
With a mission.
Or was he in silent prayer?
Did he know I was there?
I hesitated.
Did it make sense
To disturb his silence?
The planes were now gone
Bomb craters smouldered on,
Cordite fumes clogged the nose,
Still he retained his pose.
My God . . . He was so still
Fear gripped this searching soldier.
so:
I touched him on the shoulder.
He toppled forward . . .
Dead . . .

Bill Ridley

D-DAY SOLDIER

The 'Duc de Normandie' sails
away from family beaches
which once
were Omaha and Sword,
transports me from the history
which you will never leave.
I pause to pray;
thank you for your legacy of freedom
to come and go;
picture the still corner of Hermanville
where your 21 years have lain for 50 more;
sense again the rose
which flowers in your dust.

Like a Guy Fawkes rocket showering white stars
against a matte black sky,
sun drops explode,
diamond bright,
illumine the crepe silk surface
of the dark sea.

Hilary Tinsley

NO MANS LAND OF WASTED SOULS

God resides in no mans land,
And tries to stop the slaughter,
A destructive waste of life and limb,
The outcome of mans greed and sin.

Only when the fight is lost,
Prayers are said by men of cloth,
Prayers and thoughts redeem the loss,
Perennial memorials count the cost.

God in spirit still resides,
Unknown soldier cross inscribed,
No mans land was never gained,
It is levelled to ease the pain.

Admired, the architects work is done,
Memorials built for brother, son,
Graveyard workers toil untired,
Rows of plants to be admired.

Rod Marshall

TO BE CONTINUED

Ten million losses during world war one,
How many we wondered, for ours.
And if - when we alas had gone -
Would anyone send *us* flowers?

In Africa, who took care of us
Glad of a copper or two?
Taking Life slowly with never a fuss,
Times would change - they knew.

Fifty years hence that cause was won,
The emergence of one brand new nation.
Yet - other *'wars'* have again begun.
Beware of jubilation.

Charles White

SOLDIER

Soldier, tooled up ready,
Waiting for the enemy,
Out of sight, finger on the trigger,
Mind drifts off to family scene,
Wife with kids, smiling faces,
Happy scenes in summer garden,
Shattered by grenade exploding,
Shocks soldier into action,
Possessed by survival instinct,
Shoots - to stay alive,
Shoots - to see friends at campfire breakfast,
Shoots - for lift home,
Shoots - for family reunion.

Alan Pollard

YOUNG PHILIP'S WAR

There's barbed wire on English seafronts
We thought the Germans would invade
No-one can understand the reason
Why it was delayed

Now Allied forces landed on French beaches
Forever to be known as D-Day
There were some heavy losses
It seems it was the only way

We see Germans on the newsreels
Their faces look so grim
Perhaps they really know now
That they will never win

Last night Churchill made one of his speeches
We agreed with everything he said
My father only spoke when it was over
Come on, it's time you children went to bed.

Pauline Kavanagh

WORLD WAR II

The call up came
Every one did something
The cry your country
        Needs you
The battle was fought
In the air on land and
        sea
The bombs did drop
The men fought a fierce
        Battle to
Stop the enemy
Lives were lost
Home and abroad
The sky was dark
As planes roared
Overhead
Some never made it
But the fight had
to go on
For our freedom
So thank you God
For letting us
Be Free.

Eileen Kisby

'ANT! TANK'

Detachments rear, attack, attack,
'Tiger tank, just down the track,
Follow orders, make no fuss,
Get that tank, before he gets us!

Sight on the turret, Gunner Black,
Knock it out, Lest he fires back;
One shot, my boys, is all we've got,
One shot from him, we've had our lot!

Well fired lads, hit square on,
The things on fire, the turrets gone.
the blokes inside had no chance,
Sacrificed in a field in France.

Ron Duck

REMEMBRANCE

It had been a clear sun warmed day
you khaki clad, and me in summer print,
we walked on moorland, sheep grazed,
a skylark sang, and our native village
in the valley looked so peaceful.
You picked a wild orchid and gave it
to me, boy and girl in love, such
sweetness, youth brimmed with future plans
we did not speak of death, but
it lurked in the shadows black.
That last embrace, before you boarded the train, both
being brave at our involuntary parting, I watched
your waving hand fade into nothingness.
Autumn shed its leaves and by Christmas
came, you had gone forever, John.

E M Pucknell

THE CENOTAPH

The Cenotaph Memorial
Reminds of those who died
Who fought for our dear country
Their courage not to hide
In Whitehall we remember
Forever and a day
In Whitehall standing solemn
together as we pray.

Melvyn Roiter

PRICE OF FREEDOM

Wall of concrete,
Scene of hate,
Stone witness cold,
Watches death unfold.
Trying to flee,
To be free,
Bullets fly,
Too numb to cry,
Blood flows red,
A boy lies dead.

Too young to die,
Why, why, why?
Is it real,
Death I feel.
An innocent boy,
Seeking - freedom - joy.
High price to pay,
No other way.
life is past,
Freedom at last.

Rachel Murray

A GARDEN OF REMEMBRANCE

As roses burst through iron gates
so memories come rushing
through our defence
their growth thrives
though we grow old
and adds a dimension
that we must sense
there is no pruning
no cutting back
no choice that we can make
the garden of remembrance
will continue to survive
while we mortals
live out life's span
and play our part
in the Universal plan.

Tamar Segal

THE BATTLE COURSE

In Blighty before '44
There were Battle Courses galore.
Live bullets flew and dummies bled,
And plastic heroes calmly led.
Oblivious they to shot and shell
They knew the aim was off full well.
These actors on the heaving stage,
Did scorn all fear with persiflage.
But later when the aim was sure,
Their actions had a strain less pure.
The certain ending of the play that day,
Was fraught with doubt and unalloyed dismay.
Off came the masque, off the buskin wraps,
They were revealed less brave than wiser chaps.

James Stevenson

EARTHLY POWER

With eyes confused and wide in fear
Strangers now to joy and tear
She looked at me as if I'd know
Just where to run, which way to go

A child abandoned, hurt, in pain
Lying in the mud and rain
Made me pray for Earthly power
To make me master of the hour

I asked for strength that I might run
Away from tank and murder's gun
Carry her so far that she
Might share a safer place with me

When suddenly the stable ground
Rose in the air with bursting sound
Boulders, mud, and searing flame
Lifted up this child of Cain

Stripped away her future years
Tomorrow's joys and childhood tears
And made me wonder if God cared
Or listened to one single word.

John Parkin

HIROSHIMA; AN AUGUST MORNING

A flash of light seared the sky,
Mr Tanimoto had a distinct recollection
It travelled east to west, city to hills,
Like a sheet of sun, a flashing sword.
There was time to react, time to feel fear.
He bellied up hard against rocks in a garden,
He heard no roar, (no-one recalls hearing noise.)
In panic, not thinking, silent and dazed,
Running and running, through dust clouds,
A dust city under a silent sky,
        burning buildings
and burning flesh, living bodies,
skin sloughed off -
he stumbles, torn by a shriek,
'humans. these are humans!
flesh rises before him like grinning smoke
        from the ash.
Chanting for sanity
        for a way through the panic,
before the hard rain, a whirlwind, a miasma, a gas tank
        burned
and Mr Tanimoto saw his reflection in the river
        from Taiko Bridge.

Bill Dancy

ONE LANCASTER

We watched them flying weapons of war
On an English summer evening
Young men gallant and brave
We wished them well as they flew overhead
and prayed for their safe return
Night after night in the sunset glow
they roared across land and sea
Fifty years on we are reminded of
the sacrifice they made
One Lancaster bomber, some of the few
who fought and won for us all.

Marian Marks

TO THE UNKNOWN

Allow the eye of the Soul to see, to follow a star
Stifle it not with anger, let not hatred penetrate so far,
that it's clear, yet mystical Ray of hopeful light,
Is again and again, turned for so many into dark obscure night.

Our heritage of beauty, ever overthrown, when ever there is war,
The Rose forgotten, because it's Poppy Time once more,
yet still Truth struggles on to find it's way,
to lead out of fear and death to a more God-given day.

Creator of the flowers, could we but learn from thee,
To keep the hearts compassion, that was always meant to be,
showing the only way to defeat the enemies of love,
And holds the secret to discover, the message of the Dove.

Those that remain in the Poppy's opium of forgetfulness, live still,
The Rose speaks, 'Forget-me-not' There is that which will fulfil,
The Hearts desire, which lies not in the Poppy, but with everlasting Rose,
'Man Proposes - God Disposes' we will, but it is His Will alone, that knows.

I Gunner

TO BE FORGIVEN

Call out the names
Assembled here, on stone parade,
With such a nice precision.
'Their Glory lives' -
Dear God,
It does, but so our follies do!
This mortal sin -
Of waste, of broken life,
Of beauty crushed -
Will not be healed or hid
By half the truth.

So, trumpeter -
Put searing end to silence time
With flame of sound ascending.
Be pitiless:
Play on,
Till, roused, these stumbling dead present
Their foulest wounds,
For our live tears to wash.
Then, undeceived,
We may acquaint with fault -
And be ashamed.

Paul Hampton

SPIRIT OF WAR

A still made up of shining metal, flesh and seed;
A flame ignite of hatred, politics and greed;
A mix of good and evil in the pot consigned,
An incandescent flux of pain and loss entwined
Boiling wildly still-bottoms rising to the top,
Asylums run by inmates raking off the crop;
All fanned by chancers' venom waiting to be spilled;
Death and glory, heady spirit of war distilled,
Flower of youth, inflame, intoxicate, recruit
Like forests full of blossoms bursting near to fruit,
Performing deeds of valour far above review,
Willing leaders in sacrifice and payments due
And those that did not fall know well it was by chance
And mourn those left behind when anthems stopped the dance
And mourn the babies never now conceived and born
To drink perhaps the heady spirit, brew of war,
Simmering! simmering!

Jeff Friar

MEMORIES OF WAR

An East End child not yet in my teens,
What did I know of politicians ways and means.
Britain and Germany are going to War!
What on earth are they doing that for!

But one learns quickly in days of youth,
Soon barrage balloons flew high above our roof.
Anderson shelters erected in our garden,
Gas masks issued, Mickey Mouse ones for children.

Then came the bombers, each and every night.
High explosives and incendiaries to light
the skies, which filled with smoke and dust.
Fear for the lives of loved ones was the worst.

Young men fought in far off lands, too many died.
many were maimed, crippled, blinded, and I cried.
For with the years came better understanding,
we had to stop what the enemy was demanding.

But surely there has to be some other way,
better than all this blood letting, for one day
our young ones will only feel that might is right,
and this old world will be become dark, with no
redeeming light.

Joyce G Shinn